The Clearing

THE WALT MCDONALD FIRST-BOOK SERIES IN POETRY

Robert A. Fink, *editor*

Burning Wyclif, Thom Satterlee

Slag, Mark Sullivan

Keeping My Name, Catherine Tufariello

Strange Pietà, Gregory Fraser

Skin, April Lindner

Setting the World in Order, Rick Campbell

Heartwood, Miriam Vermilya

Into a Thousand Mouths, Janice Whittington

A Desk in the Elephant House, Cathryn Essinger

Stalking Joy, Margaret Benbow

An Animal of the Sixth Day, Laura Fargas

Anna and the Steel Mill, Deborah Burnham

The Andrew Poems, Shelly Wagner

Between Towns, Laurie Kutchins

The Love That Ended Yesterday in Texas, Cathy Smith Bowers

The Clearing

Philip White

Introduction by Robert A. Fink

Texas Tech University Press

This book is typeset in Stempel Garamond. The paper used in this book meets the minimum requirements of ANSI/NISO Z39.48-1992 (R1997). ∞

Designed by Jennifer E. Holmes

LIBRARY OF CONGRESS CATALOGING-IN-PUBLICATION DATA

White, Philip, 1962-
  The clearing / Philip White ; introduction by Robert A. Fink.
    p. cm. — (Walt McDonald first-book series in poetry)
  Summary: "Focusing on transformations of love and self over time and in bereavement. White's subjects are autobiographical—love, marriage, the deaths of his father, mother, and, more centrally, his first wife. Questioning memory and self-deception, the poems employ language and metaphors drawn from ordinary life. Winner, Walt McDonald First-Book Competition 2007"—Provided by publisher.
  ISBN-13: 978-0-89672-605-5 (alk. paper)
  ISBN-10: 0-89672-605-3 (alk. paper)
  I. Title.
  PS3623.H57874C55 2007
  811'.6—dc22
                          2006033642

Printed in the United States of America
07 08 09 10 11 12 13 14 15 / 9 8 7 6 5 4 3 2 1
TS

Texas Tech University Press
Box 41037
Lubbock, Texas 79409-1037 USA
800.832.4042
ttup@ttu.edu
www.ttup.ttu.edu

For
Fred G White
Patricia Moody White

For
LeeAnne Smith White

Acknowledgments

Grateful acknowledgment is made to the editors of the following publications, in which some of these poems first appeared:

Antioch Review: "Idyll," "Sepia"
Cumberland Poetry Review: "Family Prayer"
Fine Madness: "The Minnows"
Hudson Review: "A Muffled Sound"
The Journal: "Lament," "Red Branch," "Baucis and Philemon,"
    "The Fires," "Birdhouse"
Literary Imagination: "Movietime"
New England Review: "Wings"
The New Republic: "They Rise"
Ninth Letter: "Veil"
Quarterly West: "Solstice," "Keepsake"
Sewanee Review: "Cape Meditations," "East Lawn," "Dog Days"
Southeast Review: "Train à Grande Vitesse," "Herb Garden,"
    "Threshold"
Southern Review: "The Afternoon," "Vine"
Southwest Review: "Why Orpheus Looked Back"
Tar River Poetry: "At Dead Horse Point," "Heron"

The author wishes to thank the editors of *Poetry Daily, Verse Daily,* and *Pushcart Prize XXXI,* who selected some of the poems for their publications, and Centre College for its generous support.

Thanks also to the many family members and friends who have given encouragement. Special thanks are due to the late Leslie Norris and LeeAnne Smith White; to Timothy Liu, Kathy Fagan, John Hollander, and Joshua Mehigan; and most of all to Lisa Briana Williams.

Contents

Introduction

The bedside phone rings at 3:00 a.m. A somber newscaster inter-
rupts our situation comedy to bring us this special bulletin. A man
in uniform knocks at our door. We have all hesitated before lifting
the receiver; all sat up from the couch, back muscles tightening; all
of us have paused, dumbstruck, when the officer "coughing at the
door, / our name in hand" ("Loving Again"), glances down to be
sure, then asks his easy question.

This is the "news we don't turn on or off, / that seeks us out"
("Loving Again"), reminding us again that we and our loved ones are
fragile, human after all. Emily Dickinson calls this moment the hour of
lead— "Remembered, if outlived, / As Freezing persons, recollect the
Snow— / First—Chill—then Stupor—then the letting go—" ("After
great pain, a formal feeling comes"). Philip White's *The Clearing* is
about this letting go, about the *afterlife*—not the life of the dead raised,
as the apostle Paul wrote, "incorruptible" (1 Corinthians 15:52), but
the life of the spouse who did not die and now must somehow go on
living the life that comes after the loss of a loved one. *The Clearing* is
not a book about dying; nor does it outline a manageable progression
from mourning to healing. It is a book about living "the endless years
strong in feeling" that "lie here now inert around" a young husband
who has lost his wife and also his mother and his father ("The
Afterlife").

The opening poem, "Cricket," asks the question the persona strug-
gles to answer throughout the book: "Whose life is this? / And was it
the dead who left it, or we?" The husband and wife are so entwined,
"knotted" ("Aubade"), the persona, even years after his wife's death,
seems unable to know himself apart from his wife. Is it possible for
him to call in "builders" ("Cricket") to construct a new life, his after-
life? This is no stereotypical quest for healing. The mourning husband
wants to let go "of all / the falsehoods about death I've told"; he would

speak in grief's "distant language, / without pity and without anguish" ("Threshold"). He would use words, poetry, as a spell ("Family Prayer") against false emotion, contrived meaning. We all know loss changes us. The persona of *The Clearing* can acknowledge by the end of the book that after the loss of love, "we will never find ourselves again" ("Six O'Clock Flight to the Interment"), never find that comfortable sense of self we knew before being awakened to, opening the door to, the afterlife.

The Clearing is arranged in five sections, the first of which introduces the husband-persona's conflict, his desire to stand, for a moment, outside of time, only "a flutter in the vast wave that is not toward anything at all / at this instant, even oblivion" ("Idyll"), and speak "quietly" to his wife "and believe everything" ("Wings"), accepting change, the known world leaving him, "turning into / something new" ("The Minnows") the persona is seeking to define apart from his wife. He asks, "Tell me my story, love; / how could I know it, we are such knotted things" ("Aubade"). The past and the present seem one, "a dazzle of light," the busy old sun rising and setting— "severing, amnesiac, / that sublime impertinence" ("Where We Are"). The persona begins his existential quest to know himself, aware, now, that marriage was not, as he and his wife thought, "the end of the story" but rather "the fraught climax" ("Aubade"). *The Clearing* examines the extended denouement.

Section II looks back to the loss of the persona's mother and father and the shelter they provided—a loving, safe, spiritual childhood—and posits a central question of the book: Does one grow numb to grief, accustomed to loss, forgetful of a face? Now that the persona has lived to see his past before him, has his eye been "ground dull or ground clean" ("At Dead Horse Point")? Is "Truth . . . the first casualty / of survival" ("Magnolia")? Can he, and should he, continue to grieve and mourn for his parents and his wife, "the dream forever looping" ("Movietime"), speaking to them in his "calm, / matter-of-fact way" ("Raptor"), retaining the flash, savoring it, that balm-soothing neglect of time? Will he be unfaithful if he forgets?

The central image of III (which focuses on the loss of the persona's wife) is that of the old, faithful couple Baucis and Philemon—the image of "linden and oak twining / together as one" ("Baucis and Philemon"). This image is reinforced in "The Clearing," title poem of the book, with its woods of "interlocking maple, birch, / pine" surrounding a "space of shafting light" illuminating the "great beech" tree—wrinkled, creviced, bent, and dry but from its "center an explosion / of limbs in air," symbol of ramification; but the myth of Baucis and Philemon and the life-from-seeming-death symbol of the old beech tree cannot serve for the persona and his wife. Unlike Baucis and Philemon, the persona and his wife were not granted their wish to grow old together and die together. Now the persona's "trunk" is "still bent around this vacancy, / holding the shape of it" ("In the Leaves"). Now, like his deceased wife, he, too, is "a shadow with you here in this other life" ("Keepsake")—the afterlife, where, the persona acknowledges, "Nothing is given," and he "must choose how to turn / his head, what to look at, where to land" ("Crow") as he seeks to know and speak the truth of loss, grief, and mourning, "wanting to take / each thing in, not knowing what part would be lost / that I might struggle into this life again" ("East Lawn").

In IV, his transition into this new life leads the persona to a philosophical, existential point of view recognizing that "even mind-changing sorrow dribbles away" ("Magnolia"), and "we get / neglectful" of our dead, bringing the persona to his overwhelming question, "Is the real thing possible?" ("Magnolia"). His mourning has reached the stage at which he can acknowledge being "dissatisfied, craving entry / into some life or other. . . . But where to go?" ("The Bookstore in Town"). If we "grow used" to sorrow being "misplaced, shouldered out by some new thing / clamoring into presence" ("Magnolia"), how can we know and tell the truth of grief and mourning—that "there is no absence our mind cannot match" ("Dog Days"), "no solace, no wisdom, no code"; life can be *good* but not *happy* ("Vortical"). And when we come to love again, what we have already learned will be forgotten, and we will have to relearn "what it is to be lost / and found and lost everlastingly" ("Loving Again"), but at least being "found" means we *will* come to love again.

In the final section, the persona can declare, "The poem is done, has struck / and foundered. . . . No one was saved" ("The Spice

Trade"). The persona as Orpheus looked back for Eurydice, thereby losing her to the Underworld, not because he was too impatient to see his beloved again, but because the world he saw before him, "coming back," was the "blank, evacuated gaze" of absence—the gaze "that wants nothing / yet embraces all we do" ("Why Orpheus Looked Back"). He sang for his lost love, knowing that the afterlife only permits looking ahead to tomorrow and tomorrow and tomorrow already turning "to sand between your fingers" ("The Afterlife"). The final poem, "Six O'Clock Flight to the Interment," does not leave the persona, and us, in despair. He can say, "I feel both freed and lost." The strands to his past, his deceased parents, and his late wife "hardly hold together anymore / or hold me to what's gone." His loves have fallen from him, and even his pain is gone, but this is not a sign of healing, at least not for him: "It's ugly feeling nothing, but worse / to be unaware of it, or to call it *moving on* / or *working through* or *healing.*"

From the start of the book, the persona has sought to speak quietly and profess only what he has discovered to be true, mocking neither himself nor us by insisting that "nothing at all had been lost or the lost / were only what they seemed to us to be" ("Six O'Clock Flight to the Interment"). Truth is, Philip White's persona concludes, "in time the mind numbs / and wanders, and the dead don't come." He also acknowledges that "there's room for joy here, too." Though after the death of one we loved, we can never be our innocent selves again, and the guilt of having forgotten we are temporary will accompany us all our days, we, the ones who did not die, can choose our new way, choose how we spend our days—living, moving on into the afterlife, a kind of affirmation, a kind of joy.

Robert A. Fink
Abilene 2007

The Clearing

Cricket

A frigid morning, the trees outside nearly
leafless so the ticking now is limb on limb,
a few ice grains slithering on metal flashings,
roofers scraping shingles a block away, wind
hollowing out some other space to be here.
And some of the dead rustle back, bodily,
hunching out in the cold just as they did.
I approve the particular ways they shoulder
the burdens of themselves, remember by feel
the knot to the side of one's spine where the pain
never stopped, note this one's voice: she had a snap
inside her coat sleeve once that chirped exactly
like a cricket when it touched her watchface;
I'd listen for it as she moved along creaking
in spite of herself, laughing. Whose life is this?
And was it the dead who left it, or we? We close
our eyes and someone vanishes, open them
and another life is there to be seen. Time
for a new roof, someone thinks, and calls in
builders, an odd, unplaceable, wind-blurred
rasp at dawn. At first I thought it was a man
out in the cold trying futilely to clear
his throat, about to speak. But it went on
and on. It was only the builders out there.

I

Wings
for l.s.w.

You never got where you wanted.
How in the story the man always
pulled away, as in the dream
of childhood that didn't change.
You wrote, "I'm still afraid."

When you were young over the river,
leaning on the rail, then
wind filled your hair
and the concrete buttress became
a prow spreading the water.

What have I done but live
by this heart and its bag of tricks?

If I say, Light fell
from your body, or, Hundreds
of leaves burst into wings, forgive me.
I want to speak to you quietly
and believe everything.

1989

Daylilies

You've seen them late in the season,
spumes of spear-shaped leaves
from a clutter of brick
at roadside, or under a broken lintel
the spent, upraised stems
stiffening toward completion.

These make no seed and therefore
build to no end but beauty.
Nor bloom by their own chances
but by the will of some woman who knelt
when the cabin still stood
and buried haggard rootstalks with her hands.

They are her desire.
Think of her
when she saw the petals first fall open,
when she felt herself
for one moment never
more frail, powerful, alive.

The Minnows
for Mike and Tracy Graff

The minnows under the bridge are lost
    in the ruse of their own bodies.
Dylan, crouched over them, holds

    his breath, waits for them to show
themselves by moving. His father
    and I stand a few steps off

in the goldenrod, talking, distracted—
    I absorbed in the color of the sun
flushing the alders, and he glancing

    off at the house where his wife
now rests, a child—what is it,
    asleep? dreaming?—in her side.

When I look over, he's saying someone
    we both love is in pain,
changing, that the world we know

    is leaving us, turning into
something new. The sun is still
    high, but yellowing. Dylan,

who has already sensed the presence
    that will displace him, squats
over the stream, his mind fixed

    on the minnows. Invisible now,
any minute they may or may not move
    into another life. The delay is

exquisite, unthinkable. In the quiet
    braid of the stream the light
is unraveling; the minnows remain

    beyond knowledge, perfectly still.

Idyll

You sprawl beside me in a lawn chair looking through the catalogue
for movies you want to see. The sky above you is a pane so blue

the house beneath it seems childish, comical, a little ark filled
with your touches. Everything is in motion. The fields

around us part and wave, isolate tufts of white rush over the trees.
Looking up, for an instant I am cut adrift, watching the arms

of the pear tree twined and chafing like the arms of those
who have loved for a long time, the leaves around them in torment,

bowing and bowing. Does it matter that two jets have made an X
over the house, diverging, that beside me a spider has spun its nest

in a crown of dead flowers, a brown, abstracted fleur-de-lis
from last year, that we are only a part of what is happening,

a flutter in the vast wave that is not toward anything at all
at this instant, even oblivion? By now you have moved

up the hill behind me, following the sun, every now and then
exclaiming unintelligibly: A title? A story line? My name?

Little startling outcries. But when I look, you are not hurt
and do not want me and have not even lifted your eyes.

Train à Grande Vitesse

A small, pleasurable lurch of beginning.
Paris, but it might be any big city—

eighteen rails sunk in cinder, high
stone walls crowned with chainlink,

the stretched, Euclidean ganglia
of wires overhead, a zinc gray dawn.

Then a feeling of thinning and sooner
than we think, openness, the old countryside.

Time to sail through small stations
(a man smoking, a woman folding a magazine),

and after long emptiness, time
to come upon the ancient village:

sunstruck white terra cotta buildings,
a broad terraced hillside where a few

figures bend over vines as they have
for centuries, an order of rooms

and streets and fields in which people
have dreamed, spoken of idle things,

fallen silent. Is there a name for this?
The wheels turn. White towns

full of life rise up out of trees
and as quickly recede. After centuries

of thought our suspension is flawless.
We no longer need to feel anything.

For moments we can believe we are outside
it all, hurled along in our silver car.

Cape Meditations

1. A Brightness

Sun floods the gritty pots
in the strict embrasure.
My face upturned;
you in the next room
curled in sheets.
I can't move, held by
the light of another spring
breaking through me.
Your body like leaves,
like marble. All
that we have been.

2. Off-Season

Tulips in the jar and the perfect rooms.
The sea in the window a haze
of darkness rustling over sandhills.
Unsteady wind, raincloud, saltrose, tarnish.
Afternoon in bed thinking about it.
The shifting possibilities.
Love like bread. Distance. The sea pounding
or silent. The sun crossing a thousand times.

3. Rented Cottage

Stunted pine and beach grass darkened
with gusts of rain. Stinging wind.
For three days we lived on bread, cold
sunlight spreading across our plates.
We stood in a gale till our eyes

ached. The water below us churned,
shifting color. The book we'd read
said the sea had been fatal there,
hands had clutched in idle embrace,
eyes locked on the site. But for us
who would leave, it was food, color, light.
The mind built in that ravaged place.

Mesa Verde

Pinyon country, sagebrush, big sky.
Even at eighty the distances
are inhuman. We doze through the world
of old westerns; your brothers in back,
finishing their mysteries, curl
into sleep, want something to eat.
Then the turnoff, the enforced
stall as switchbacks reel us up
the escarpment to the high plain;
at last the dusty, ill-lit
gift shop, the land-bureau maps
marking the way to the site.
We find the ruins as pictured
but to our wonder child-size,
and linger in rooms where life
is for a moment suddenly
imaginable, then make way
for the next group. On the rocks
we tip back, watch buzzards wheel
above us. They can afford
patience. The wind that swept
the tiny square rooms and lifted
the hair of the Anasazi dead
will swallow us soon enough.
Back in the car, backtracking.
First, the starved sublimity
of desert, then boredom again,
hunger. Outside, whizzing by,
the gunned-out, forsaken trailers,
the dead cars and lights of Cortez.

Where We Are

The café is nice—airy, light, giving
on trees, the street—
but someone two tables down
is unpacking his grief.

We feel, of course, violated,
though we've been there,
the distance between us
and him, say, four
hundred rinsings
of the face, erosion
our daily bread.

Yet where we are an agony holds us.

—And a dazzle of light
from chrome passing
outside; the sun again,
severing, amnesiac,
that sublime impertinence.

Aubade

Quaintly virginal, we thought marriage
the end of the story; not the fraught
climax, nor this, plotlines in time painfully
crossed that will not end except in age
or sorrow. Still, clarity comes: I wake
into the light, your hair before my eyes
a wave of darkness, your arm thrown
over you like a child, and I remember
tenderness, that old knife, and all the pains
you have put in my care. Even in sleep
our bodies seek each other, your face the moon
lighting my dreams. And by day, scenes beyond
untanglement. Tell me my story, love;
how could I know it, we are such knotted things?

Threshold

All morning the empty boats in the cove
        drift on their lines with the tide's flow.
     I sit by the window at the chipboard table

writing what happens, letting go of all
        the falsehoods about death I've told.
     Outside, the door at the office groans open:

voices through the wall, women, men,
        speaking as if in tongues, in pure tone.
     Now laughter, the door again, tools clattering

down; hammer blows, clapboards being pried at,
        a ripsaw in spasms, shattering, abrupt.
     What if every day were like this, someone

building, someone tearing apart. What if
        under the white paint there were nothing
     but wood, held together by nails

and screws. Centuries would pass and no one
        would notice. The boats would ease and lift
     out in the blue cove thousands of times,

and over them, ceaselessly, the gulls
        would cry in their distant language,
     without pity and without anguish.

II

At Dead Horse Point

Abraded landscape: the great forgotten
seabed around me, and at my feet
a huge, jagged gash ripped
by millennia of wind and inconstant rain
laying bare the vivid layers.
I came here as a child once, played
while my parents gazed. What they saw
I can't say. Maybe some death
was made theirs by magnitude,
true desert, as in time their deaths,
grief on grief, were mine. Yet I've lived
to see my past before me and ask
if the eye is ground dull or ground clean
that it can lean like this into vacancy,
gorging on laceration and light.

Sepia

West at Nephi, then rabbitbrush, sage,
hills of dust white for miles, or streaked,
sudden with iron, bloody. We'd follow
the dry river to the hive-shaped brickkilns
abandoned from pioneer times, then steer
south five miles into cottonwoods—Oak City:
the old tire swing, an air dead and still.
Before us the ancestral house, empty
except for beds, a guest book, and a wall
of nineteenth-century faces, crimped,
impenetrable, like those of—not heroes,
but the very poor. And stretching out
and away from it, a vast, open frame
that mother filled from memory so dutifully
it became our memory, steeped in sepia,
monochrome: Here the frivolous, bent-iron
fence, and here great-grandmother in a swatch
of cheap floral print, smile composed, mildly
ironic, the roses ("a hundred kinds!")
flowering at her side. And beyond her,
westward, the same blank horizon we'd had
before us all morning, three hundred miles
of heat-warp and dust, the road simmering off
into colorlessness, and for a time
something far and indistinct that pushed
its way into it, that flashed, we thought,
maybe once, and then was never seen.

Family Prayer

Our knees ached, the rug cut its tight
braid in our skin, yet circled there,
eyes bowed and closed, we felt our lives
knit in words, night and morning
the cadenced phrase holding the mind.
Habits of the soul die hard, but die.
We know more of damage now
and evil: lives shredded by time
or, worse, the kind that blossoms back
behind the trouble in the mind,
the routine cruelties, pacts made
with shame and rage, the daily
weave of grief muffling it all.
Who will guard them now, that chaste couple
and those children with just a twinge
of pain starting to tear between
their shoulder blades and only words
like spells to keep them safe from harm?

From the Country of the Sun

Like other lights, our sun flares and passes.
What luck then, mother, that we were ever here,
that we rose to it daily, unthinkingly,
putting on our clothes, tying our laces
as someone taught us to, forgetting again
and again the heaviness of our bodies.
I remember your visit east, the big cities.
You were girlish, I thought, even then,
like Miranda in her new world: "Such creatures!"
I almost hear you say. And your rapture
when you finally saw the sea, the brazen
everyday glare on the wet sand, and you
standing there scarcely containing your joy,
still strong enough to make a shadow.

Raptor

One day my hawk was gone. There was space
at the top of the pole where most mornings
I found her. The next few months I looked
in the other places, then came back and stood
under the pole where when I drew close
she would shift to take me in or launch out
soundlessly above me, turning to keep me
in sight at an angle, low, at perfect ease,
moving only feathers at the very tips
of her wings. I stood, looking up, alone.
This was in Ashfield, a different state,
maybe eight years ago, yet she hangs still
in the air above me, moves when I move.
She changed my mind. I knew the animal
without illusion, but sometimes as she turned
above me I would speak to her in the calm,
matter-of-fact way I had come to speak
to my mother and the others who had gone.

Herb Garden

Somewhere deep in summer a man tends
a tiny plot of herbs. Dense crests of rosemary
spill over the rocks beneath him, the marjoram
he touches is in tight, minuscule bloom.
The man is ill, in a week he will die,
and for this reason his fingers move slowly
through the dark soil, over the curling leaves,
calming his mind. We do what we have seen done:
mornings grow long, frost darkens, and one day
I bend down, bury small plants to the stem.
A man works alongside me, his hands
delicate and wide like mine laying open
the soil, pressing it down around the starts.
I know he carries death in his body.
I hear in his breath the slightest moan.
When the pain is too great, he rests for a while,
stands over my shoulder, silent, watchful,
until he is gone, until he is lost in the thought
of a boy turning in his mind the leaf shapes,
the beautiful names: *savory, sweet balm, thyme.*

The Roads

Five o'clock, barely morning. For now
I lie in the darkness, thinking, waiting.
On a morning like this my father died,
lay back in his room, the blank ceiling
reflecting his gaze. What I remember
is a photograph of his I found once,
a curving lane, arching yellow trees,
a house. I wanted to have seen that.
I took his old Leica and went out
in the yard. Everything offered itself,
the cut bark of the pear trees, sunlight
in the broken fence, rippling leaves, pores,
lines, textures. None of it came through.
My pictures seemed cramped, blurred, closed-in.
Not like his. His were calendar scenes,
of course, old phrases of light, but enough
to say, he stopped here, struck by something;
huge skies opened before him, and the roads
grew thin, doubled back into the trees.

Heron

Once, out walking, I came suddenly over a crest
onto a slow bend in the Charles.
I had not known the river was so near.
In the dark under the lip of foliage on the far bank
I saw, when my eyes came to themselves,
my first night heron, hunched, black-
crowned, trailing two elegant long white plumes.
It was the end of something.
I had driven as far east as I could drive.
The love I had followed would, in weeks, fail.
I had been running too long from my dead father.
I did not know who I was.
When the bird moved, I knew all of this.
It had an awkward grace there by the river
lifting its body into silence of another order.

Movietime

The sound is lost, but the place, long sold, comes
ticking back. There we are in the workroom
downstairs at grandpa's, standing for the camera,
for grandpa's rigorous directing eye.
There we stand, summoned to be visible
forever, fidgeting therefore, trying
to pull ourselves together, breaking at last,
as if out of sheer nerves, into song.
Make no mistake, it is discomfort we feel
to be caught here, mouths opening and opening
without avail, like the gates of ivory, horn.
We can go back, we sometimes feel, or we can't.
Or we *are* back, the dream forever looping,
the eye finding again the human eye,
every voiced note a chord suspended
over years, only the sound really is
lost, and some of us are ghosts already.

III

East Lawn

Behind me, just far enough off that I could hear
voices, men were digging; a dangling chain
rang fitfully. Snow had fallen, and in the sun
the mountain rose, blinding and serene.
One low dark cloud rode across its face;
shadows, haggard and without shape, spilled
over the clefts and folds. The light was still
a memory then, the tufts of scrub oak, sage,
everything her eye had touched once in the rapt
pang of attention that was hers. I stood alone
where I had stood in the fall, months earlier,
with the families and children, flowers in hand
over the open grave. First the flowers were thrown,
then the earth. I remember the rich incremental
dark by shovelful smothering their flaming colors
like a cloudbank slowly blotting out stars.
And as the earth fell, my heart finally failed
and I cast my eye around wildly, wanting to take
each thing in, not knowing what part would be lost
that I might struggle into this life again.

l.s.w. 1965–2001

Lament

My heart stopped,
but my body went on.
Love, have mercy on me.
The sky was ash,
the earth a cinder.
I don't know why I lived.
I walked up fifth street.
I walked up fifth street.
My face became a stranger.
I woke in chambers
with others around me,
sat down amid joy,
ate without hunger.
My body went on,
my face a stranger.
The sky was ash.
I ate without hunger.
My love died,
but my heart went on.
I don't know why I lived.
Love, have mercy on me.

Vine

That year, at the party we threw for our friend's birthday,
before I brought the cake in streaming with flame
and before the dancing started, before we stood around,
ice clinking in our glasses, and talked with too much zest
about the clever meat favors someone had spent
the afternoon assembling, I was out in the backyard
by the woods, caught by the trailing arbutus, or rather
by the shadow of the trailing arbutus on the crumbling
foundation of a defunct shed. Something in that play
of sun and air, some curve in the shadow of some
curling vine, took me to the light of an afternoon
before any of this, before the woman I loved had died.
Then the friends arrived and we filled our plates
and glasses and talked as we'd hoped, half our words
lost in the music, the movement of our bodies in time.
Then I went in and lit the candles and grasped
the cake with its corona of flames in both hands
and walked toward our friend, carefully, as if afraid
of spilling. The dancing stopped and everyone sang
at once and when I held the cake out to him our eyes met
and in that weird light I saw my own face, how hard,
for his own reasons, he was trying to be happy.

They Rise

All things die . . . all things but grief. And so they rise,
they who are left, into the old, old dawn,
whose fingertips just have power to graze them.

They rise in the gray and rose and grow watchful.
They know that all of it must go and the rays
that remain remain an insult to those

that didn't stay. And so they stay, and suffer
division, and grasp what they can of the living
and the dead and the old, old fingertips of rose.

Red Branch

A terrible fidelity
held me. I had to move
to keep quiet. Limbs
plunging in the wind,
dark air hollowed, shot
through with promise
of snow, I sought you.
Absence swept the fields.
At a bend, spiring
redcedar, cold, down-
licking brands of bared
sumac. Like you
they kept beckoning,
kept burning and not
burning, held their tongues.

Braid

Now, when I can't find you, I'm most afraid.
I feel I must hack through the hours I've lived
without you as through some growth occluding
my path, must lever myself back to relieve
eclipse. In the dim slip of times all I hear is water,
slurred, dissolving, obsessive. And your face,
pained or desiring, beyond me even then, rises
into and out of vision like the glittering weft
on the reaches behind me where the channel bends.

A Muffled Sound

You'd loved it as a girl, the peaked loft high
in Colorado, the window there, the quiet
as dark, sweeping limbs bowed outside.
You wanted me to see, as if then I might
understand. How neatly you'd cleaned for us,
yet still the spiders in the sheets left welts,
and I'd forgotten till this morning how I'd
hurt you there: so young I hardly knew
my mind or how to speak to another.
I learned, in time I learned. But for what?
I'm only half here. This muffled sound, it's not
us crying, talking it out. If the cabin
still stands, outside your window gold pollen
ghosts across the pines for someone else.

Baucis and Philemon

As in the fable, linden and oak twining
together as one, yes; but before that
and after, two in pain who found themselves
up late, talking. Our portal of escape
became a language we could not talk
our way back through, tongues, like limbs
and trunks, having fused in the passage:
nights in the nest, days, the bed made, unmade,
and memory growing thick around it, tangled
with dreams like flames driving streaks upward
through our leaves and veins. So when the gods
of endings came, we made a place even
for them inside, and when they asked, no need
to speak, we knew already what our wish was . . .
Never to grieve? Never to let suffer?
Impossible, then, to say who broke faith.
In the end we could not save the other:
there was one pain, one fraying braid, and two
tracing the snapped threads back, trying to mend.
Then there was one on the bed, up late, talking.

Keepsake

We had our days, didn't we—sun-stained,
hand-rubbed, pieced and plighted in some massing tale
I'd just begun to see the pattern of.
But we were the birds, too, starving in the woods,
ravening up the crumbs we dropped behind
till we were utterly lost (there was that failed
love, a music box you couldn't fix and I
couldn't, our griefs jangling us, dividing).
Where did you go, wood nymph, your huge, hurt eyes
that saw too much, fluttering in the weeds?—
You always moved moth-wise: sudden juttings, gusts,
exaltations, long self-banishing silence.
Come back to me sometimes. I wander now too,
am a shadow with you here in this other life.

The Clearing

The homely wrinkled torso, creviced, bent,
dry, and from the center an explosion
of limbs in air, a great beech occupied
that space of shafting light we'd stumbled in
from the shade of interlocking maple, birch,
pine. It tinged our minds, raised in us
its likeness, towering fountain of fixed
purpose, image of what inexorably is . . .
You, whose word then made me see, have vanished.
So long your absence has inhabited me
I hardly know where my own death begins.
And the green blazing in your eye that day?
A blank night builds in me now. It will have
the tree, its power to stand, to ramify.

The Fires

You took yourself from us, love. Why?
The part of me that knew your pain once thought
it knew; now I founder. There was a fault
in me that shifted, the strata disaligned;
your lips, arms, eyes, the way you held your face
up to the wind in fierce concentration,
how do these pertain now? and to whom?
I have lived, as you wanted, loved again.
Yet feel the snow on one slope of the mountain
has slipped and all the trees I knew there
mangled, shorn—Wood for the new fires?
How terrible . . . these nights lying awake late
trying to explain what happens in this world
to our children, who were never born.

Veil

All morning on the fringe of memory a song
that deepened these woods for me in summer
has kept itself. Now snow brings out the lines
of hills, trees: the dense bramble in fine
drypoint and, nearer, dark turns of limb made clear
by contrast, a gash before me in the ground
as if the burin had slipped. Everything
in terms of others, I'm thinking, brought over,
veiled, the way a thing you said got tangled
with a sparrow's song I loved when you were gone.
Sometimes what I remember is itself
a memory, forged in some earlier need,
and the thing—a catch of pain in your face,
your capacity to surprise—gets scumbled,
blocked out. Bare fact, true, can be hard:
nights we lay, you reading, I trying to keep
from being swallowed, from losing my thought.
Yet I loved that too, the tug of us inside
the other, growing old, chafing maybe,
knowing we would have to begin again,
but not yet, not yet. And I almost have it,
that promise of a morning held out before us,
your thought humming, known, mysterious,
like a voice quietly, deeply there, far back,
beside me those nights as I drift asleep.
Then you reach, turn out the light, and I
am in some woods again, stumbling ahead;
around me birdsong, haunting, half-familiar,
and behind, the mundane regress, branch
behind branch, the lost faces, the lost thread.

In the Leaves

Figuring, disfiguring, love made me one,
this trunk still bent around this vacancy,
holding the shape of it. In bed alone
with the one I loved, on streets with others
alone, our laughter drawing the lines, in rooms
for years, it seemed, not needing to speak,
secure in the silence between; and then, what?
a ripple in the leaves, too small to be seen . . .
How deep are the seeds of calamity?
As deep as peace, your love beside you?
Something is happening in a far place.
An end is finding a means. A sentence
is forming. Someone will suffer. There is
so little we can do for one another.

The Afternoon

Having arrived at this place
in the day, you wonder
what to make of light
stealing across countertops,
vases, walls, light so far
into the known it feels like
erosion, old glacial shift.
Now is the moment,
you think, of nothing
called for, no mystery
beckoning. Somewhere
the heart drew back in its
scrapheap, eyes grew full
of sleep, desire dulled.
What to do with the longing
still to be gathered in, or up?
How fix this mirror
that finds you always
as you were made
to believe, the object
of adoration, hieratic,
clarified? Stroll awhile here
in the dahlias, something
tells you, light dripping
from leaves repetitively.
To the hard absence apply
the salve of forgetfulness
that eats away anything. Now

is the time, it urges, to garner
the fragments of earthenware
or dear glass your spade
turns up digging the new path.
Or let them fall back.

Solstice

Every morning is the morning after a massacre.
Here, in midsummer, the spindrift fleabane
froths the hills and insect song
swells steadily from the fields at noon.
Dark lofting pines luff in warm air.
On the fringes, where the grass is mown,
a few children play makeshift games
or practice holding their breath under water.

Crow

Awake early, walking, a man looks up
at a crow in flight, notes for the first time
the exact but minutely adaptive arc
the shouldering wings describe. He feels it
in his arms, the strain, the oaring stride,
his chest a prow dividing the warm
morning air. Around, shops opening, noise
of trucks and cars. How long has the man
been out walking? How many years,
for unchangeable reasons? Then one morning
a crow picks across a colorless sky
and he understands. Nothing is given.
The man also must choose how to turn
his head, what to look at, where to land.

IV

Magnolia

For three weeks, thrumming early summer rain,
thoughts cycling to the erratic rhythm.
Now, morning sun, warm breeze through one window,
then through the window on the other side;
heavy air perfumed partly with fresh shoots,
partly with rot, life in another form.
Even mind-changing sorrow dribbles away,
gets misplaced, shouldered out by some new thing
clamoring into presence. We grow used
to it, this being at war, meaning we get
neglectful. Truth is the first casualty
of survival: close your eyes and you'll reach
one lucky day de facto tranquility.
Is the real thing possible? Po Chu-i
had his demons—poetry, any old wind,
his daughter at play before her death
tangling him in illusion, love always
coming to grief. And the sages, Seneca,
Epictetus, they had Rome to forget,
no wonder they embraced renunciation.
Pain will grip me too again, will cinch
once more the snarl of my thought tighter.
Not now, not these few minutes, weeks, years.
For now I try to place this odor entering
at the window, that glimmer through the leaves,
some flesh-colored blossom in slow wilt.

Dog Days

Near stasis on the porch. When I move, my dog
looks up. I've called what's there in his eye love,
but now it's suddenly the look I watched
drain out in a dog's eyes at roadside once:
pure animal mind, ready for what might come
(a pat? a run? food? rest?), without knowledge
and therefore without fear and without death:
a fire guttering in a wilderness
with no one there to see. I saw. For us,
there is no absence our mind cannot match.
We feel at times like an empty sleeve in wind
or a stone blind in its own density.
And love? It may strike us as an undertow
that drags us from ourselves beyond our depth,
or just dog love: "Next?" it says, raising its eyes.
It varies. We who have lived by the millrace
of reflected days and brought our minds
to bear the space between atoms and stars
and seen our natures change must choose which way
we take our time. Are we empty or full?
In the right place? Here, in the neighborhood,
how casually our loves look up at what called
them forth, or fade away like this dry dusk
that leaks from us and leaves us wanting more.

Birdhouse

The swallow can't say who made the perfect space
he lives in. It's all to spec, though, the soft pine
cut and drilled by some schoolchild with designs,
dreaming, no doubt, of bluebirds. I remember
how that was. The child didn't think to nail
the box somewhere *off* the path, but the swallow
doesn't mind or wasn't thinking himself
when he hunkered with his mate gripped by more
pressing demands. Mornings, he stands at his door
swiveling his well-built head, assessing my threat
perhaps, though by now I like to think he knows
who I am. Wonder? Fear? The meanings
are crossed, but we nod at each other as I pass . . .
I think, if god is what's beyond us, then bird
and man, to the other, might be divinity—
me with my misplaced loves and notions of dying
stars and vast spaces cold past imagining.
It all goes on anyway, the swallow not
giving it a thought. We live in drifts
of radiant excess from the sun, which would kill
or blind if not for our filter of ozone
and small-mindedness, building perfectly
to code our little rooms, shading ourselves in,
making it all substantial, nodding perhaps
a bit warily at the sun as it passes.

Vortical

"Life is good," I tapped out, after two years
of silence, despairing of words. Almost
too soon, my friend tapped back, "I'm so glad
to hear you're happy." What I meant was
a northern harrier this afternoon stopped
in air, tucked, and found a chute I couldn't see
through a mesh of bare trees. And higher,
four redtails rode an updraft effortlessly,
hardly tilting to look down. And higher,
a few dots I guessed were vultures turned
in slow vortex, ever higher, blinking
like the eyes of the very old, no relation
to me, no solace, no wisdom, no code.

Fragrant Harbor

Above me a chasm of livid sky opened,
black cumuli rushing past on either side;
down the hill, my latest town, the evening lights
of tire stores, stockyards, church lots flickering on.
It was like the stray boatlights flickering on
across the harbor of an island city
where I stood at wharfside once, young, alone,
looking out, millions of strangers behind me,
at the far mountains then in chance brilliance,
the storm clearing and dark, tearing clouds
underlit, as tonight, with lavender and saffron.
I hardly think of those years anymore,
but the fetor of the wharf came back, the brine
and gasoline and rotting fish, with a sense
of what had brought me, filial luck and faith,
a vision still intact but crossed with gusts
of severance, my father far off at home
dying, and thoughts, new thoughts, my own,
that would bring me here, just starting to form.

The Bookstore in Town

I'm in Magazines, looking for what counts
this month as poetry. In back, a vault
of windows frames the night, sky and town
a seamless black. Between, as if hung in air,
a cloverleaf ramps more to loiter here
like me, dissatisfied, craving entry
into some life or other. But there are
so many, and the talk is loud and small,
words I couldn't live in for long. And all
the unbought to truck off month by month . . .
"Plow it under," I say aloud, surprising
myself. But where to go? Outside, the cars
stream like blips, like corpuscles, tiny
beams thrown ahead of them into the dark.

Geodes

for l.b.w.

Suddenly the redbud burst along its boughs,
the drab finch was gold again and black, back
in bloom anyhow, and we were close, close.

But how far will this take us, we with lives
already at our backs, with silences our words,
no matter how peaked, won't break, can't keep?

I think of the stones we found in the woods,
those lumpish clods you liked, with nodes
cracked and bulging (you said) like eyes: *geodes,*

we called them, "little worlds," and that was that.
Yet how could we know what we held
but did not break open? Let them be, we said,

clouds fretting vacant, buried heads, petaled
gales, seasons, atmospheres, whorls in whorls.

Oriole

Down the hillside cataracts of flowers,
out on the headlands the seawind keening,
in the mute street looking, sniffing, listening,
a child opens his mouth around a word:

oriole. Years pass, then two bicolored birds
riffle through the leaves of your mimosa;
swifts like sickles and scissoring nighthawks cut
the sky in pieces. *Look up,* you say. *That.*

But I look down at the stream, blue shards
tumbling in the furrow. My days are seas,
terrible at the fringes: *turbulent vermilion,*
you say, painting the underside of heaven,

then, *oriole!,* and over tidal solitudes
the blue-gold dome rings like something told.

Isola

The isle of love, or Circe's isle, they call it.
After so much history, we can't say.
We've come to talk, to make plans or let go.
But one day in the rooms above the cove

and everything slows down. The arguments
of the past fall away. All we want
is to stay on this wind-gouged, flowering brink
finding words or not, sipping something

strong, taking it in, the gulls teetering midair
or plummeting out of sight, a late, pared moon
drizzling the sea-lanes, and in the morning

the island boys and girls on motorinos
riding a wave of magma that crested here
oh about two million years ago.

Loving Again

What we learned once we'll have to learn again.
Who could live as if every good-bye were the last?
We look at this or that to keep from seeing
the air around us. There are eyes behind these.

And there is news we don't turn on or off,
that seeks us out, that interrupts the lunch.
An officer stands coughing at the door,
our name in hand, and when all that's finally done,

there's not silence so much as a pause filled
with what's missing, what we already knew.
We're that old dent in the mirror glass
we learned not to see, the scribbled address,

the heirloom pen, the ring, what it is to be lost
and found and lost again everlastingly.

V

The Afterlife

They lie here now inert around you,
the endless years strong in feeling,

like snails that gave out mid-path,
life evaporated from their coils,

crusts so freed they weigh nothing
and turn to sand between your fingers.

The Palisades

Once there was something called moss. I seem
to remember someone sitting on a rock
growing used to rest and turning slowly
into moss. Someone else, I think, stumbled
into a pit or cistern—it gets hazy here:
a hand goes up behind a rim, then drops
down fast, like a rock. Another refused
to go on, whatever was said. Someone
gave out at the partially caved-in stile,
someone at the point where one tire rut stopped.
Only a few of us were left when we got
to the river, which seemed to grow wider
and deeper as we watched. We would need help
getting across. Had any of us, we tried
to remember, come from the other side?
We sat on pieces broken off from the rock
outcrops around us that we'd somehow
come down, from peering steadily at which
while our eyes absorbed the darkening
alkaline light one of us started naming
the ages. Each word took in a million years.
There was rock and water and air the color
of rock and water. Our outlines blurred.
A gap opened, one of us began. *Someone
fell in a hole,* another said. Our voices
were like gravel against the sound of water.
It was a long time before the last
of us decided what to call the river.

Why Orpheus Looked Back

Even her voice is soundless now. She moves
like the damselflies in honeysuckle leaves
along the stream, their torsos iridescing,
wings so black they seem fluttering rents
in the tangible scene: so much silence
fringing every word, so much dark around
each wavering gleam. But what else could I
have asked of absence? I had seen its world,
the blank, evacuated gaze that wants nothing
yet embraces all we do. It was the world
I saw before me, coming back. I sang then
not for it but her, fainter though she'd grown
than air. I looked back because I knew
whichever way I looked it would be there.

Revenant

In full sun a splash of red flower on a white retaining wall.
Still I'm not here. Love of this rips us into the hereafter,
memory is a kind of death. In the corner of the eye others
loiter, having lost their lives apart from us, mute,
recidivist, moonstruck rifts, the black wake spreading behind.

Cinnabar

Saltmarsh grass, feather
of a wren, alder cone.
We won't find them here.

Nothing will come again.
Only the bodily catch
on the dragchain,

the haul of day
without us pulling through.
Of the few leaves one or two

of cinnabar, enough
to light someone,
stunned, glimmering, into its own.

The Spice Trade

The poem is done, has struck
and foundered. The work
of the tide has begun.

On white shoals, miscarried
belongings are arrayed
as if for sale.

The raised harbors?
The teeming bazaars?
No one was saved.

The curved hull rocks,
the myrrh of other dusks
in its hold.

Six O'Clock Flight to the Interment

Sometimes it seems that everything's dislodged,
slipping, and all we really know is pain
coming back, along perhaps with glimmers
of places we have been, made visible
by change or changed attention. As, lifted now
through brief turbulence into this routine
sublimity, I feel both freed and lost,
and see the embryonic moon in its swirl
of fluids wobble in inhuman view,
the clouds below like the very earth but scraped
and colorless, a blank moraine, a surface
infinitely formed and varied but by strictures
that elude me. *Illusion* of a surface,
I should say, because they are only clouds.
There's room in this cabin to forget them, though,
and the crude thrust forward that unanchors us.
We can close the windows and sleep, or try
again to feel what we feel, or try not to.
I'm going to see my second mother lowered
in the ground, beside her daughter, my late wife,
and in the pause I try to trace strands back
that hardly hold together anymore
or hold me to what's gone. I have to face
what is at last a limit if not a failure,
the points at which my loves fell from me
and even my pain was lost and what remained
was a mere place, the fields I walked in day
by day. It's ugly feeling nothing, but worse
to be unaware of it, or to call it *moving on*
or *working through* or *healing*, to mock ourselves
with snapshots, memories, adjusting the focus

and sentiments to suit our needs, as if
nothing at all had been lost or the lost
were only what they seemed to us to be.
Pain may be true, but in time the mind numbs
and wanders, and the dead don't come. Instead,
random places, the small dark gap in the arms
of the pine that looked inviting from inside
my first grade classroom, or the flat in Hong Kong
where I lay some mornings taking in the tops
of trees below me on the street that seemed
so disappointing but so real, though the spot
I then lay is now two hundred feet in the air
between new buildings. But sometimes simply being
someplace is all we need, and in bare sunlight
on a wall we sense a signature of what is
conducting us, arraying, granting us
entry, moving us from love to love.
After all there's room for joy here, too.
I try to piece it together, the rocky hill
where the body will be laid, the various cries
and yawps of birds that breed or pass over,
the trees in all seasons, the eroding cliffs,
small tufts or shifting atolls of cloud,
and always the vagaries of light on the cusps
of everything, and a face, maybe, something said.
But why so little of that, of others, here,
of their way of being in this place, of what
they made of the look of things that stopped us,
wrapped us in wonder, from which we took our cues?
As if they were mere scenery, props,
or like that bird back home whose call I knew
too long for it to stay with me; so lost
it was in my surroundings that only drifts
of tone, of rhythm, will come until I find

my way back to that place. But weren't they
more than that? Weren't they themselves sometimes,
maybe from the start, a world for us, a field,
and so the dead are like a struck stage, a slate
wiped clean, a cloud moraine above or below
or within which everything takes place
and we will never find ourselves again?

Selected by Robert A. Fink, *The Clearing* is the sixteenth winner of the Walt McDonald First-Book Competition in Poetry. The competition is supported generously through donated subscriptions from *The American Scholar, The Atlantic Monthly, The Georgia Review, Gulf Coast, The Hudson Review, The Massachusetts Review, Poetry, Shenandoah,* and *The Southern Review.*